Abraham Lincoln

Lincoln's Anecdotes

Abraham Lincoln

Lincoln's Anecdotes

ISBN/EAN: 9783337401979

Printed in Europe, USA, Canada, Australia, Japan

Cover: Foto ©ninafisch / pixelio.de

More available books at **www.hansebooks.com**

LINCOLN'S ANECDOTES:

A Complete Collection of the Anecdotes, Stories and Pithy Sayings of the late
Abraham Lincoln, 16th President of the United States.

OFFICE OF PUBLICATION, 105 FULTON STREET, NEW YORK.

THE AMERICAN NEWS CO., 121 NASSAU ST., N. Y., GENERAL AGENTS.

EXPLANATION TO THE READER.

The universal curiosity to see all the stories told and the numerous pithy sayings uttered by the late Abraham Lincoln, 16th President of the United States, has induced the publisher to have the present collection prepared. It embraces, he believes, all the authentic anecdotes and stories and is probably the first publication ever made exclusively devoted to Humorous Stories delivered by a Chief Magistrate under circumstances so remarkable and which impart to them an extraordinary interest. They will be read and re-read by thousands and tens of thousands all over the world, now that they are thus brought together in a convenient form.

LINCOLN'S ANECDOTES.

"Takes His Own Life."

THE compiler of the "Dictionary of Congress" states that while preparing that work for publication, in 1858, he sent to Mr. Lincoln the usual request for a sketch of his life, and received the following reply :

"Born, February 12th, 1807, in Harden Co., Ky.

"Education defective.

"Profession a lawyer.

"Have been a captain of volunteers in Black Hawk war.

"Postmaster at a very small office.

"Four times a member of the Illinois Legislature, and was a member of the Iowa House of Congress.

Yours, &c.,
A. Lincoln.

How He Earned His First Dollar.

"I WAS about eighteen years of age," said the President.   "I belonged, you know, to what they call down south "the scrubs ;" people who do not own slaves are nobody there.   But we had succeeded in raising, chiefly by my labor, sufficient produce, as I thought, to justify me in taking it down the river to sell.

"After much persuasion, I got the consent of mother to go, and constructed a little flatboat, large enough to take a barrel or two of things, that we had gathered, with myself and little bundle, down to New Orleans. A steamer was coming down the river. We have you know, no wharves on the Western streams ; and the custom was, if passengers were at any of the landings, for them to go out in a boat, the steamer stopping and taking them aboard.

"I was contemplating my new flatboat, and wondering whether I could make it stronger or improve it in any particular, when two men came down to the shore

brother asked me what I did that for. I told him I
didn't want the old horse bitten in that way. "Why,"
said my brother, "*that's all that made him go !*" "Now,"
said Mr. Lincoln, "if Mr. ———, has a presidential *chin-
fly* biting him, I'm not going to knock him off, if it will
only make his department *go.*"

The Hoop-less Girl.

A POOR girl in a scanty but neat dress, came to him
one day imploring forgiveness and pardon for her
brother, who had been sentenced to be shot, for deser-
tion. "My poor girl," said he, "you have come here
with no governor, or senator, or member of congress,
to plead your cause. You seem honest and truthful;
and you don't wear hoops, and I will be whipped, but I will
pardon your brother."

———

"WHAT do you think Mr. President, is the reason
General McCloud does not reply to the letter from the
Chicago Convention ?"

"Oh !" replied Mr. Lincoln, with a characteristic
twinkle of the eyes, "*he is intrenching !*"

A Blunderbus.

SPEAKING of President Polk quoting a certain opinion of Jefferson's he said : That this opinion of Mr.
Jefferson, in one branch at least, is, in the hands of Mr.
Polk, like McFingal's gun, "Bears wide and kicks the
owner over."

Won't Treat His Driver.

"I WAS once travelling out in Illinois, when my driver
halted his team before a tavern."

"Goin' to treat, Mr. Lincoln," said John.

"I do not drink," said I, not wishing to be detained
at such an early stage of my journey.

"Let me have a chew, then !"

"I never use tobacco, my friend."

"Look a here, sir," said he. "If a fellah has no
small vices, I have always noticed that he makes up for
it in big ones."

Root Hog or Die.

"AMONG the stories freshest in my mind," says Carpenter in his entertaining sketch, "was one which he

related to me shortly after its occurence, belonging to the history of the famous interview on board the *Race Queen*, at Hampton Roads, between himself and Secretary Seward, and the Rebel Peace Commissioners. "You see," said he, "we had reached and were discussing the *slavery* question. Mr. Hunter said, substantially, that the slaves, always accustomed to an overseer, and to work upon compulsion, suddenly freed, as they would be if the South should consent to peace on the basis of the "Emancipation Proclamation," would precipitate not only themselves, but the entire Southern society into irremediable ruin. No work would be done, nothing could be cultivated, and both blacks and whites would *starve!*" I waited for Seward to answer that argument, but as he was silent, I at length said : "Mr. Hunter, *you* ought to know a great deal better about this matter than I, for you have always lived under the slave system. I can only say, in reply to your statement of the case, that it reminds me of a man out in Illinois, by the name of Case, who undertook a few years ago, to raise a very large herd of hogs. It was a great trouble to *feed* them, and how to get around this was a puzzle to him. At length he hit upon the plan of planting an immense field of potatoes, and, when they were sufficiently grown, he turned the whole herd into the field, and let them have full swing, thus saving, not only the labor of feeding the hogs, but also that of digging the potatoes ! Charmed with his sagacity, he stood one day leaning against the fence, counting his hogs, when a neighbor came along. "Well, well," said he, "Mr. Case, this is all very fine. Your hogs are doing very well just now, but you know out here in Illinois the frost comes early, and the ground freezes for a foot deep. Then what are they going to do ?" This was a view of the matter, Mr. Case had not taken into account. Butchering-time for hogs was way on in December or January ! He scratched his head, and at length stammered out. "Well, it may come pretty hard on their *snouts*, but I don't see but that it will be ' *root hog or die !* ' "

Colonel Moody's "Little Story of Andy Johnson."

"I had a visit last night from Col. Moody, ' the fight-

ing Methodist Parson,' as he is called in Tennessee. He
is on his way to the Philadelphia Conference, and, being
in Washington over night, came up to see me. He told
me this story of Andy Johnson and General Buel, which
interested me intensely. Col. Moody was in Nashville
the day that it was reported that Buel had decided to
evacuate the city. The rebels, strongly re-inforced,
were said to be within two days' march of the Capitol.
Of course the city was greatly excited. Said Moody, "I
went in search of Johnson, at the edge of the evening,
and found him in his office, closeted with two gentlemen, who were walking the floor with him, one on each
side. As I entered, they retired leaving me alone with
Johnson, who came up to me, manifesting intense feeling, and said, "Moody, we are sold out! Buel is a
traitor! He is going to evacuate the city, and in forty-
eight hours we shall all be in the hands of the rebels!"
Then he commenced pacing the room again, twisting
his hands, and chafing like a caged tiger, utterly insensible to his friend's intreaties to become calm. Suddenly
he turned and said, "Moody, can you pray?" "That's
my business, sir, as a minister of the gospel," returned
the Col. "Well, Moody, I wish you would pray," said
Johnson; and instantly both went down upon their
knees, at opposite sides of the room. As the prayer became fervent, Johnson began to respond in true Methodist style. Presently he crawled over on his hands and
knees to Moody's side, and put his arm over him manifesting the deepest emotion. Closing the prayer with
a hearty "Amen" from each, they arose. Johnson took
a long breath, and said, with emphasis. "Moody, I
feel better!" Shortly afterwards he asked, "will you
stand be me?" "Certainly, I will," was the answer.
"Well, Moody, I can depend upon you. You are one
in a hundred thousand!" He then commenced pacing
the floor again. Suddenly he wheeled, the current of
his thought having changed, and said: "Oh! Moody,
I don't want you to think I have become a religious man
because I asked you to pray. I am sorry to say it, but
I am not, and never pretended to be religious. No one
knows this better than you; but, Moody, there is one

thing about it—I do believe in Almighty God ! and I believe also in the Bible, and I say *damn* me, if Nashville *shall be surrendered ! And Nashville was not surrendered !*"

No Influence.

JUDGE BALDWIN, of California, solicited a pass of General Halleck one day. "We have been deceived too often," said Halleck, "and I regret I can't grant it." Baldwin applied to Stanton with the same success. He then solicited it of Mr. Lincoln. "Have you applied to Halleck," inquired the President. "Yes, and met with a flat refusal," said the Judge. "Then you must see Stanton," continued the President. "I have, and with the same result," was the reply. "Well, then," said Mr. Lincoln, with a smile, "I can do nothing ; for you must know *that I have very little influence with this Administration.*"

Dan Webster's Dirty Hand.

ON the occasion of a Sunday School procession pass ing the North side of the White House reviewed before Mr. Lincoln, he told the Hon. Mr. Odell the following :

"I heard a story last night about Daniel Webster when a lad, which was new to me, and it has been running in my head all the morning. When quite young, at school, Daniel was one day guilty of a gross violation of the rules. He was detected in the act, and called up by the teacher for punishment. This was to be the old-fashioned "feruling" of the hand. His hands happened to be very dirty. Knowing this, on his way to the teacher's desk he *spit* upon the palm of his *right* hand, wiping it off upon the side of his pantaloons. "Give me your hand, sir," said the teacher very sternly. Out went the right hand, partly cleansed. The teacher looked at it a moment, and said; "Daniel, if you will find another hand in this school-room as filthy as that, I will let you off this time." Instantly from behind his back came the *left* hand. "Here it is, sir," was the reply. "That will do," said the teacher, "for this time. You can take your seat, sir !"

"Major General I Reckon."

A NEW levy of troops required, on a certain occasion,

the appointment of a large additional number of brigadier and major-generals. Among the immense number
of applications, Mr. Lincoln came upon one wherein the
claims of a certain worthy (not in the service at all),
"for a generalship" were glowingly set forth. But the
applicant didn't specify whether he wanted to be brigadier or major general. The President observed this
difficulty, and solved it by by a lucid indorsement. The
clerk, on receiving the paper again, found written across
its back, "Major General, I reckon. A. Lincoln."

The Long and Short of It.

It is said that on the occasion of a serenade, the President was called for by the crowd assembled. He appeared at a window with his wife (who is somewhat be-
low the medium height), and made the following "brief
remarks:" "I am here and here is Mrs. Lincoln. That's
the long and the short of it."

The Second Coming of Our Lord.

Soon after the opening of Congress the Hon. Mr.
Shannon from California, made the customary call at
the White house. In the conversation that ensued, Mr.
Shannon said "Mr. President I met an old friend of yours
in California last summer, a Mr. Campbell, who had a
good deal to say of your Springfield life." "Ah!" returned Mr. Lincoln, "I am glad to hear of him. Campbell used to be a dry fellow in those days," he continued. "For a time he was Secretary of State. One day
during the legislative vacation, a meek cadaverous man
with a white neckcloth, introduced himself to him at
his office, and stating that he had been informed that
Mr. Campbell had the letting of the hall of representatives, he wished to secure it, if possible, for a course of
lectures he desired to deliver in Springfield. "May I
ask," said the secretary, "what is to be the subject of
your lecture?" "Certainly," was the reply, with a very
solemn expression of countenance. "The course I wish
to deliver is on the second coming of our Lord." It is
of no use," said C., "if you take my advice, you will not
waste your time in this city. It is my private opinion
that, if the Lord has been in Springfield once, He will
never come the second time!"

More Pegs than Holes.

SOME gentlemen were once finding fault with the President because certain Generals were not given commands. "The fact is," replied Mr. Lincoln, "I have got more *pegs* than *holes* to put them in."

Don't Cross Fox River until you get to it.

A CLERGYMAN from Springfield, Illinois, being in Washington early in Mr. Lincoln's administration, called upon him, and in the course of conversation asked him what was to be his policy on the slavery question. "Well," said the President "I will answer by telling you a story. You know Father B——. A young Methodist, was worrying about Fox River, and expressing fears that he should be prevented from fulfilling some of his engagements by a freshet in the river. Father B. checked him in his gravest manner. Said he : "young man, I have always made it a rule in my life not to cross Fox river till I get to it !" "And," added Mr. Lincoln, "I am not going to worry myself over the slavery question till I get to it."

John Morgan's Death.

BEING informed of the death of John Morgan, he said: "Well, I wouldn't crow over anybody's death ; but I can take this as *resignedly* as any dispensation of Providence."

The Emancipation Question.

A DISTINGUISHED public officer being in Washington, in an interview with the President, introduced the question of emancipation. "Well, you see," said Mr. Lincoln, "we've got to be very cautious how we manage the negro question. If we're not we shall be like the barber out in Illinois, who was shaving a fellow with a hatchet face and lantern jaws like mine. The barber stuck his finger in his customer's mouth to make his cheek stick out, but while shaving away he cut through the fellow's cheek and cut off his own finger ! If we are not very careful, we shall do as the barber did !"

Don't Shake the Rope.

AT the White House one day some gentlemen were present from the West, excited and troubled about the commissions or omissions of the Administration. The President heard them patiently and he replied :—"Gentlemen, suppose all the property you were worth was in gold, and you had put it in the hands of Blondin to carry across the Niagara River on a rope, would you shake the cable, or keep shouting out to him Blondin, stand up a little straighter—Blondin stoop a little more —go a little faster—*lean a little more to the North*—*lean a little more to the South*—No, you would hold your breath and your tongues, and keep your hands off until he was safe over. The Government are carrrying an immense weight. Untold treasures are on their hands, they are doing the very best they can. Don't badger them. Keep silence and we will get you safe across."

"Pegging" Away.

BEING asked by an "anxious" visitor as to what he would do in "certain" contingencies—provided the rebellion was not subdued after three or four years of effort on the part of the Government—"Oh," said the President "there is no alternative *but to keep "pegging away."*

About Slavery not being Dead.

AFTER the issue of the Emancipation Proclamation, Governor Morgan, of New York, was at the White House one day, when the President said :—"I do not agree with those who say that slavery is dead. We are like whalers who have been long on a chase—we have at last got the harpoon into the monster, but we must now look how we steer, or, with one "flap" of his *tail*, he will yet send us all into eternity !"

Jack Chase.

DURING a public "reception," a farmer from one of the border counties of Virginia, told the President that the Union soldiers, in passing his farm, had helped themselves not only to hay, but his horse, and he hoped the President would urge the proper office to consider his claim immediately.

Mr. Lincoln said that this reminded him of an old acquaintance of his, "Jack Chase," who used to be a lumberman on the Illinois, a steady, sober man, and the best raftsman on the river. It was quite a trick, twenty-five years ago, to take the logs over the rapids ; but he was skillful with a raft, and always kept her straight in the channel. Finally a steamer was put on, and Jack was made captain of her. He always used to take the wheel, going through the rapids. One day when the boat was plunging and wallowing along the boiling current, and Jack's utmost vigilance was being exercised to keep her in the channel, a boy pulled his coat-tail, and hailed him with—"Say, Mister Captain! I wish you would just stop your boat a minute—I've lost my apple overboard !"

About Explaining Matters in the Newspapers.

THE President was once speaking about an attack made him on him by the committee on the conduct of the war for a certain alleged blunder, or something worse, in the South-West—the matter involved being one which had fallen directly under the observation of the official to whom he was talking, who possessed official evidence completely upsetting all the conclusions of the committee.

"Might it not be well for me," queried the official, "to set this matter right in a letter to some paper, stating the facts as they actually transpired ?"

"Oh, no," replied the President, "at least, not now. If I were to try to read, much less answer, all the attacks made on me, this shop might as well be closed for any other businesss. I do the very best I know how—the very best I can ; and I mean to keep doing so until the end. If the end brings me out all right, what is said against me won't amount to anything. If the end brings me out wrong, ten angels swearing I was right would make no difference."

Illegal Writs.

A GENTLEMAN was relating to the President how a friend of his had been driven away from New Orleans as a Unionist, and how, on his expulsion, when he asked to see the writ by which he was expelled, the deputation which called upon him told him that the Government had made up their minds to do nothing illegal, and so they had issued no illegal writs, and simply meant to to make him go of his own free will. "Well" said Mr. Lincoln, "that reminds me of a hotel-keeper down at

St. Louis, who boasted that he never had a death in his hotel, for whenever a guest was dying in his house he carried him out to die in the gutter."

Hanging a Man for Blowing his Nose in the Street.

ONE evening the President brought a couple of friends into the "State dining-room" to see Carpenter's picture when the conversation "reminded him of the following circumstance ; "Judge——," said he, "held the strongest ideas of rigid government and close construction that I ever met. It was said of him on one occasion that he would *hang* a man for blowing his nose in the street, but he would quash the indictment if it failed to specify which hand he blew it with !"

A FRIEND said to him one day after the President had told him of his purpose to make a call for more troops, "It will destroy your chance for re-election." "It matters not" replied Mr. Lincoln, "It matters not. *We must have the men.* If I go down I intend to go, like the Cumberland, with my colors flying."

Patrick's Boots.

(EXTRACT from "Speech:") To lay a duty, for the improvement of any particular harbor, upon the tonnage coming into that harbor will never clear a greatly obstructed river. The idea that we could, involves the same absurdity of the Irish bull about the new boots : "I shall never get 'em on," says Patrick, "till I wear 'em a day or two, and stretch 'em a little."

Turned Out to Root.

(EXTRACT from a speech in Congress :) The other day one of the gentlemen from Georgia, (Mr. Iverson,) an eloquent man, and a man of learning, so far as I can judge, not being learned myself, came down upon us astonishingly. He spoke in what a certain editor calls a "scathing and Beechery style." At the end of his second severe flash I was struck blind, and found myself feeling with my fingers for an assurance of my continued physical existence. A little of the bone was left and I gradually revived. He declared we had deserted all our principles and had turned Harry Clay out, like an old horse, to root. I merely wish to ask the gentleman if the Whigs are the only party he can think of, who sometimes turn old horses out to root ? Is not a certain Martin Van Buren an old horse, which your own party have turned out to root ! and is he not rooting a little to your discomfort 'bout now !

Abraham as a Warrior.

BLACK HAWK WAR.—Commenting in a Congressional speech during the canvass of 1848, upon the effects of General Cass's biographers to exalt their idol into a military hero, he thus alluded to an episode in his own life:

By the way, Mr. Speaker, did you know I am a military hero ? Yes, sir, in the days of the Black Hawk war, I fought, bled, and———came away ! Speaking of General Cass's career, reminds me of my own. I was not at Stillman's defeat, but I was about as near it as Cass to Hull's surrender, and like him, *I saw the place very soon afterward.* It is quite certain I did not break my sword, for I had none to break, but I bent my musket pretty badly on one occasion. If Cass broke his sword, the idea is, he broke it in desperation; I bent the musket by accident. If General Cass went in advance of me in picking wortleberries, I guess I surpassed him in charges upon wild onions ! If he saw any live fighting Indians, it was more than I did, but I had a good many bloody struggles with the musquetoes, and although I never fainted from loss af blood, I can truly say I was often very hungry !

Mr. Speaker, should I ever conclude to doff whatever our Democratic friends may suppose there is of black-cockade Federalism about me, and, thereupon, they should take me up as their candidate for the Presidency, I protest that they shall not make fun of me as they have of General Cass, by attempting to write me into a military hero !

Extract from Speech after the Fall of Richmond.

I propose now closing up by requesting that your band play "Dixie." I thought "Dixie" one of the best tunes I ever heard. I insisted yesterday that we had fairly captured it! I presented the question to the Attorney General, and he gave it as his opinion that it is our lawful prize. I ask the band to give us a good turn upon it.

Hatching the Egg.

CONCEDE that the new Government of Louisiana is only what it should be, as the egg to the fowl, we shall sooner have the fowl by hatching the egg, than by *smashing* it.

A Sure Dream.

"GENERAL, have you heard from General Sherman," said he to Grant.

"I have not, but I am hourly expecting dispatches from him, announcing the surrender of Johnson."

"Well," said Mr. Lincoln, "you'll hear very soon, and the news will be important."

"Why do you think so," said the General.

"Because," said the President, "I had a dream last night, and ever since the war began I have invariably had the same dream before any very important military event has occurred. It is in your line, too, Mr. Wells. The dream is that I saw a ship sailing very rapidly, and I am sure that it portends some important national event. I had the same dream on the eve of Antietam, Gettysburgh, etc.

"IF Jeff Davis is the head of the Rebellion," said Mr. Lincoln to an army officer, "Humphrey Marshall is its paunch, and Floyd and Wise its legs!"

The Democratic Ox-Gad.

SPEAKING of the unconstitutional career of General Cass in reference to the Wilmot Proviso, he said : "When the question was agitated in 1846, General Cass was in a blustering hurry to take ground for it. He sought to be in advance; but soon he began to see glimpses of the great Democratic ox-gad waving in his face, and to hear distinctly a voice saying, "back, back, sir, back a little." He shakes his head and bats his eyes, and blunders back to his position of March '47 ; but still the gad waives, and the voice grows more distinct, and sharper still—"back sir, back I say! further

back!" and back he goes to the position of December
'47 ; at which the gad is still, and the voice soothingly
says : "So ! stand still at that !"

"Boarding Out" Your Board Bill.

REFERRING to the "charges" of General Cass upon the
Treasury, he continued : "He not only did the labor
of several men at the *same* time, but that he often did it,
at several *places* many hundred miles apart, *at the same
time.* And at eating, too, his capacities are shown to be
quite as wonderful. From October 21st, to May 22d, he
ate ten rations a day in Michigan, ten rations a day here
in Washington, and nearly five dollars worth a day be-
sides, partly on the road between the two places. And
then there is an important discovery in his example—
the art of being paid for what one eats, instead of having to pay for it. Hereafter, if any nice young man
shall owe a bill which he cannot pay in any other way,
he can *just board it out!* Mr. Speaker, we have all heard
of the animal standing in doubt between two stacks of
hay and starving to death ; the like of that would never
happen to General Cass. Place the stacks a thousand
miles apart, he would stand stock still, mid-way between
them, and eat them both *at once;* and the green grass
along the line would be apt to suffer some too at the
same time. By all means, make him President, gentlemen. He will feed you bounteously—if, if, there is
any left after he shall have helped himself !"

The Rugged Russian Bear.

IN his speech at Chicago, July 10th, '58, Douglas used
this illustration : "I shall deal with this allied army
just as the Russians dealt with the allies at Sebastopol,
that is, the Russians did not stop to inquire, when they
fired a broadside, whether it hit an Englishman, a
Frenchman, or a Turk. Nor will I stop to inquire
whether my blows hit three Republican leaders or three
allies, who are holding the federal offices, and yet acting
in concert with them."

To this Mr. Lincoln replied : "Well, now, gentlemen, is not this very alarming ! Just to think of it !
right at the onset of his canvass, I, a poor, kind, ami-

able, intelligent gentleman, I am to be SLAIN in this way. Why, my friends, the Judge, is not only, as it turns out, not a *dead lion*, nor even a *living one*—he is the rugged Russian Bear! I beg that he will indulge us while we barely suggest to him that the allies took Sebastopol!"

Abraham Lincoln and His Barber.

THE Springfield (Illinois) correspondent of the Chicago *Times* contributes the following interesting reminiscence:

On a raw, cold evening in December, 1831, a man presenting the appearance of a very light mulatto, being what is technically called a quadroon, stood by the door of a log cabin in the town of New Salem, Sangamon county (now Menard), in this state. His clothing was travel-stained and considerably dilapidated; his carriage was erect; his eye clear and sparkling with the vivacity of *La Belle* France, for he was a native of Hayti, and the blood of the Creole French of that island was in his veins. The precursors of darkness began to fall upon the sombre scene, the shadow of the woods in the distance to lengthen on the snow-clad ground, while the gray clouds, surcharged with moisture, and behind which the sun was setting, admonished the solitary Creole that he must seek shelter, and that rather quickly, from the pitiless peltings of a coming coming storm.

Lifting his eyes to take another survey of the cold and cheerless prospect, he was struck by the appearance of a tall, uncouth-looking figure, emerging out of the shadow of the wood about two hundred yards from where he stood. It was that of a man considerably over six feet in height, carrying an ax carelessly slung upon his shoulder; his gait was slouching, something between a lope and a shamble; he stooped considerably; his eyes were bent upon the ground; his disengaged arm hung carelessly by his side, and, with a swinging motion, kept time to the ungraceful movement of his body; his hair and beard were long, of a jet black color and apparently unkempt; he had a red woolen cap upon his head, such as was then worn by woodchoppers, or the hired help of

farmers generally ; an old pair of blanket leggings, tied
with buckskin thongs above the knees and at the ankles,
were wound about the calves of his legs ; they were rusty
with age and ragged with use in the brushwood ; a ragged coat, once blue or black, and of coarse cloth, was
.bound with a similar thong of buckskin about his waist.
In fact, he presented the appearance of an ordinary
backwoodsman.

He stopped at the door of the log cabin, which was
the only grocery store and tavern of which the place
could boast—nodded pleasantly, after the fashion of the
day, to the Creole, and was about to enter, when the
latter asked him how far it was to Springfield. The
backwoodsman told him the distance and passed in, followed hesitatingly by the traveller. When they reached
the interior, the uncouth backwoodsman stepped over
the large oaken bench which stood in front of the fire,
laid down his ax, and, turning his back to the huge pile
of burning logs on the old-fashioned hearth, warmed
himself, stretching out his lank and long hands to the
blaze as if he enjoyed it hugely.

The man who stood with his back to the log fire in
that primitive hostelry, on that gray December evening,
was Abraham Lincoln, the future President of the
United States, and the author of the great emancipation proclamation. The stranger Creole, with the blood
of the despised African coursing in his veins, was Wil-
liam Florville, the quadroon, subsequently and for years
Abraham Lincoln's barber.

When Mr. Lincoln was about to be married he was
taken quite ill at a medical friend's house in this city. He
sent for Florville, who stayed with him some time, and
while there administered the medicine which the physi-
cian prescribed for him. About ten days afterward he
came into the shop and said, "Billy, I want you to
shave me and trim my hair also, and I want you to do it
as if I was going to be married." Billy replied, "If I
do, Mr. Lincoln, it will cost you one dollar. We charge
extra for shaving when they are going to be married."
" All right," replied Mr. Lincoln. "I suppose I ought
not to dance without paying the fiddler."

New England Rum.

A GENTLEMAN was one day finding fault with the constant agitation in Congress of the Slavery question. He remarked that, after the adoption of the Emancipation policy, he had hoped for something new.

"There was a man down in Maine," said the President, in reply, "who kept a grocery store, and a lot of fellows used to loaf around that for their toddy. He only gave 'em New England rum, and they drank pretty considerably of it. But after awhile they began to get tired of that, and kept asking for something new—something new—all the time. Well, one night, when the crowd were around, the grocer brought out his glasses, and says he, 'I've got something *new* for you to drink, boys, now.' 'Honor bright?' said they. 'Honor bright!' says he, and with that he sets out a jug. 'Thar,' says he, 'that's something new ; it's *New* England rum !'— "Now," remarked Mr. Lincoln, "I guess we're a good deal like that crowd, and Congress is a good deal like that store-keeper !"

He was Glad of it.

ON the occasion when the telegram from Cumberland Gap reached Mr. Lincoln that "firing was heard in the direction of Knoxville," he remarked that he "was glad of it." Some person present, who had the perils of Burnside's position uppermost in his mind, could not see *why* Mr. Lincoln should be glad of it, and so expressed himself. "Why, you see," responded the President, "it reminds me of Mistress Sallie Ward, a neighbor of mine, who had a very large family. Occasionally one of her numerous progeny would be heard crying in some out-of-the-way place, upon which Mrs. Ward would exclaim, "There's one of my children that isn't dead yet !"

Jake Thompson.

ON the occasion of one of his Cabinet asking him if it would be proper to permit Jake Thompson to slip through Maine in disguise and embark for Portland, the President was disposed to be merciful and to permit the arch-rebel to pass unmolested, but one of his secretaries urged that Thompson should be arrested as a traitor. "By permitting him to escape the penalties of treason," persistently remarked the secretary, "you sanction it." " Well," replied Mr. Lincoln, "let me tell you a story. There was an Irish soldier here last summer, who wanted something to drink stronger than water, and stopped at a drug-shop, where he espied a soda-fountain. " Mr. Doctor," said Pat, "give me, plase, a glass of soda wather, an' if yes can put in a few drops of whisky unbeknown to any one, I'll be obleged." "Now," continued Mr. Lincoln. " if Jake Thompson is permitted to go through Maine unbeknown to any one, what's the harm ? So don't have him arrested."

Sugar Coated.

THE July following Mr. Lincoln's inauguration he sent a message to Congress in which speaking of secession, and the measures taken by the southern leaders to bring it about, he made use of the following expression :—" With rebellion thus *sugar-coated*, they have been drugging the public min d of their section for more than thirty years."—

Mr. Defrees, the Government printer, a good deal disturbed by the term *sugar-coated*, went to the President about it. He told Mr. Lincoln frankly, that he ought to remember that a message to Congress was a different affair from a speech at a mass-meeting in Illinois—that the message became a part of history, and should be written accordingly.

"What is the matter now?" inquired the President.

" Why," said Mr. Defrees, "you have used an undignified expression in the message ;" and then reading the paragraph alone, he added, "I would alter the structure of that, if I were you."

" Defrees," replied Mr. Lincoln, "that word expresses precisely my idea, and I am not going to change it. The time will never come in this country when the people won't know exactly what *sugar-coated* means."

I jings !

ON a subsequent occasion a certain sentence of another message was very awkwardly constructed. Calling the

President's attention to it in the proof-copy, the latter acknowledged the force of the objection raised, and said, "Go home, Defrees, and see if you can better it." The next day Defrees took in to him his amendment. Mr. Lincoln met him by saying: "Seward found the same fault that you did, and he has been re-writing the paragraph also." Then reading Mr. Defrees' version he said: "I jings" (a common expression with him), "I think I can beat you both." Then taking up the pen, he wrote the sentence as it was finally printed.

Mrs. Brown's recollections of Abraham Lincoln.

"Well, I remember Linken. He worked with my old man thirty-four years ago, and made a *crap*. We lived on the same farm where we live now, and he worked all the season, and made a *crap* of corn, and the next winter they hauled the *crap* all the way to Galena, and sold it for two dollars and a half a bushel. At that time there was no public houses, and travelers were obliged to stay at any house along the road that could take them in.— One evening a right smart looking man rode up to the fence, and asked my old man if he could get to stay all night. 'Well,' said Mr. Brown, 'we can feed your critter, and give you something to eat, but we can't lodge you unless you can sleep in the same bed with the hired man.' The man hesitated, and asked, 'Where is he?' 'Well,' said Mr. Brown, 'you can come and see him.'— So the man got down from his critter, and Mr. Brown took him around to where, in the shade of the house, Mr. Lincoln lay his full length on the ground, with an open book before him. 'There,' said Mr. Brown, pointing to him, 'he is.' The stranger looked at him a minute, and said, 'I think he'll do." And he stayed and slept with the President of the United States."

How Lincoln thrashed a Bully.

WHILE serving as clerk in a pioneer "store," a bully came in and began to talk in an offensive manner, using much profanity and evidently wishing to provoke a quarrel. Lincoln leaned over the counter, and begged him, as ladies were present, not to indulge in such talk. The bully retorted that the opportunity had come for

which he had long sought, and he would like to see the
man who could hinder him from saying anything he
might choose to say. Lincoln still cool, told him that
if he would wait till the ladies retired, he would hear
what he had to say, and give him any satisfaction he desired. As soon as the women were gone, the man became furious. Lincoln heard his boasts and abuse for a
time, and finding he was not to be put off without a
fight, said—"Well, if you must be whipped, I suppose
I may as well whip you as any other man." This was
just what the bully had been seeking, he said, so out of
doors they went, and Lincoln made short work with
him. He threw him upon the ground, held him there
as if he had been a child, and gathering some smart-
weed which grew upon the spot, rubbed it into his face
and eyes, while the fellow bellowed with pain. Lincoln
did all of this without a particle of anger, and when the
job was finished, went immediately for water, washed
his victim's face, and did everything he could to allevi-
ate his distress. The upshot of the matter was that
the man became his fast and life-long friend, and was a
better man from that day. It was impossible then, and
it always remained impossible for Lincoln to cherish re-
sentment or revenge.

Mr. Lincoln's Postoffice.

NOT wishing to be tied to the office, as it yielded him
no revenue that would reward him for the confinement,
he made a post-office of his hat. Whenever he went
out, the letters he placed in his hat. When an anxious
looker for a letter found the post-master, he found his
office ; and the public officer taking off his hat, looked
over his mail wherever the public might find him.

The Strict Constructionist.

A good instance of the execution which he sometimes
effected with a story occurred in the legislature. There
was a troublesome member from Wabash county, who
gloried particularly in being a "strict constructionist."
He found something "unconstitutional" in every measure that was brought for discussion. He was a member
of the Judiciary Committee, and was quite apt, after

giving every measure a heavy pounding, to advocate its
reference to this Committee. No amount of sober argument could floor the member from Wabash. At last,
he came to be considered a man to be silenced, and Mr.
Lincoln was resorted to for an expedient by which this
effect might be accomplished. He soon afterwards
honored the draft thus made upon him. A measure was
brought forward in which Mr. Lincoln's constituents
were interested, when the member from Wabash rose
and discharged all his batteries upon its unconstitutional points. Mr. Lincoln then took the floor, and, with
quizzical expression of features which he could assume
at will, and a mirthful twinkle in his gray eyes, said :
" Mr. Speaker, the attack of the member from Wabash
on the constitutionality of this measure reminds me of
an old friend of mine. He's a peculiar looking old fellow, with shaggy, overhanging eye-brows, and a pair of
spectacles under them. (Everybody turned to the
member from Wabash and recognized a personal de-
scription.) One morning just after the old man got up,
he imagined, on looking out of his door, that he saw
rather a lively squirrel on a tree near his house. So he
took down his rifle and fired at the squirrel, but the
squirrel paid no attention to the shot. He loaded and
fired again, and again, until the thirteenth shot, he set
down his gun impatiently, and said to his boy, who
was looking on, " boy, there's something wrong about
this rifle." " Rifle's all right, I know 'tis," replied the
boy, " but where's your squirrel ?" " Don't you see
him, humped up about half way up the tree," inquired
the old man, peeping over his spectacles, and getting
mystified. " No I, don't," responded the boy ; and then
turning and looking into his father's face, he exclaimed,
" I see your squirrel ! You've been firing at a louse on
your eyebrow !"

How Mr. Lincoln looked.

IN personal appearance, Mr. Lincoln, or, as he is more
familiarly termed among those who know him best, ' Old
Uncle Abe,' is long, lean, and wiry. In motion he has a
great deal of the elasticity and awkwardness which indi-
cates the rough training of his life, and his conversation

savors strongly of Western idoms and pronounciation.
His height is six feet four inches. His complexion is
about that of an octoroon ; his face, without being by
any means beautiful, is genial-looking, and good humor
seems to lurk in every corner of its innumerable angles.
He has dark hair tinged with gray, a good forehead,
small eyes, a long penetrating nose, with nostrils such as
Napoleon always liked to find in his best generals, because they indicated a long head and clear thoughts ;
and a mouth, which, aside from being of magnificent
proportions, is probaly the most expressive feature of
his face.

As a speaker he is ready, precise, and fluent. His
manner before a popular assembly is as he pleases to
make it, being either superlatively ludicrous, or very im-
pressive. He employs but little gesticulation, but when
he desires to make a point, produces a shrug of his
shoulders, an elevation of his eyebrows, a depression of
his mouth, and general malformation of countenance so
comically awkward that it never fails to bring 'down
the house.' His enunciation is slow and emphatic,
and his voice, though sharp and powerful, at times has a
frequent tendency to dwindle into a shrill and unpleasant
sound ; but as before stated, the peculiar characteristic
of his delivery is the remarkable mobility of his features,
the frequent contortions of which excite a merriment his
words could not produce.

In fact the picture on the title-page of this collection
of Anecdotes, is a capital likeness of President Lincoln,
in a story-telling mood, taken from life by an artist who
had enjoyed his social entertainment, and was prepared
expressly to place the late President before the people
in his familiar manner, which endeared him to so
many.

Thrilling Incident in his Legal Career.

ONE instance which occurred during his early legal
practice is worthy of extended publication. At a camp
meeting held in Menard county, a fight took place which
ended in the murder of one of the participants in the
quarrel. A young man named Armstrong, a son of the
aged couple for whom many years before Abraham Lin-

coln had worked, was charged with the deed, and being arrested and examined, a true bill was found against him, and he was lodged in jail to await his trial. As soon as Mr. Lincoln received intelligence of the affair, he addressed a kind letter to Mrs. Armstrong, stating his anxiety that her son should have a fair trial, and offering in return for her kindness to him while in adverse circumstances some years before, his services gratuitously. Investigation convinced the volunteer attorney that the young man was the victim of a conspiracy, and he determined to postpone the case until the excitement had subsided. The day of trial however finally arrived, and the accuser testified positively that he saw the accused plunge the knife into the heart of the murdered man. He remembered all the circumstances perfectly; the murder was committed about half-past nine o'clock at night, and the moon was shining brightly. Mr. Lincoln reviewed all the testimony carefully, and then proved conclusively that the moon which the accuser had sworn was shining brightly, did not rise until an hour or more after the murder was committed. Other discrepancies were exposed, and in thirty minutes after the jury retired they returned with a verdict of "Not Guilty."

On the Congressmen.

As the President and a friend were sitting one day on the House of Representatives' steps, the last session closed, and the members filed out in a body. Lincoln looked after them with a sardonic smile.

"That reminds me," said he, "of a little incident.— When I was quite a boy, my flat-boat lay up at Alton, on the Mississippi, for a day, and I strolled about the town. I saw a large stone building, with massive walls, not so handsome, though, as this ; and while I was looking at it, the iron gateway opened, and a great body of men came out. "What do you call that?" I asked a bystander. 'That,' said he, 'is the State Prison, and those are all thieves, going home. Their time is up.'"

Burying Himself.

For weeks—indeed, for months—after the inauguration, the ante-rooms, halls and staircases of the White

House swarmed with office-seekers. More important public business was at times impeded by their brazen importunity, and every man who was supposed to have "influence" was beseiged day and night. It is true that one of the most important duties before the new administration was to place the machinery of government, as soon as possible, in trustworthy hands, but it was a terrible job to do so. They say that the office-seekers killed Harrison and Taylor—it was no fault of Abraham Lincoln that they did not kill him, for he listened to them with a degree of patience and good temper truly astonishing. At times, however, even his equanimity gave way, and more than one public man finally lost the President's good will by his pertinacity in demanding provision for his personal satellites. Some Senators and Congressmen really distinguished themselves in this respect. "I remember," says his private Secretary, W. O. Stoddard, Esq., who has contributed very happily to the general fund of Lincoln Anecdotes, "a saying of Mr. Lincoln's that comes in pretty well here : 'Poor ——, he is digging his political grave !'"

"Why, how so, Mr. President He has obtained more offices for his friends than any other man I know of."

"That's just it ; no man can stand so much of that sort of thing. You see, every man thinks he deserves a better office than the one he gets, and hates his 'big man' for not securing it, while for every man appointed there are five envious men unappointed, who never forgive him for their want of luck. So there's half a dozen enemies for each success. I like——, and don't like to see him hurt himself in that way ; I guess I won't give him any more."

The last clause had a dry bit of humor in it, for in good truth the honorable gentleman had had quite enough.

Lincoln "Fixed."

"WE had a meeting of the Whigs of the county here on last Monday, to appoint delegates to a district convention, and Baker beat me, and got the delegation instructed to go for him. The meeting, in spite of my attempt to decline it, appointed me one of the delegates, s᠈ that, in getting Baker the nomination, I shall be 'fixed' a good deal like a fellow who is made groomsman to the man who has 'cut him out,' and is marrying his own dear gal."

What the Democrats saw in Judge Douglas's face.

"They have seen, in his round, jolly, fruitful face, post-offices, land offices, marshalships, cabinet appointments, charge-ships and foreign missions bursting and sprouting out, in wonderful luxuriance, ready to be laid hold of by their greedy hands. On the contrary, nobody has ever expected me to be President. In my poor, lean, lank face nobody has ever seen that any cabbages were sprouting out."

What He said of a Political Defeat.

"I feel, I suppose, very much like the stripling who had bruised his toe—'too badly to laugh, and too big to cry.'"

His "little story" over the disruption of the Democracy.

He once knew, he said, a sound churchman by the name of Brown, who was a member of a very sober and pious committee having in charge the erection of a bridge over a dangerous and rapid river. Several architects failed, and at last Brown said he had a friend named Jones who had built several bridges, and could undoubtedly build that one. So Mr. Jones was called in. "Can you build this bridge?" inquired the committee. "Yes," replied Jones, "or any other. I could build a bridge to h—l, if necessary." The committee were shocked, and Brown felt called upon to defend his friend. "I know Jones so well," said he, "and he is so honest a man, and so good an architect, that if he states soberly and posi-tively that he can build a bridge to—to—the infernal regions, why, I believe it; but I feel bound to say that I have my doubts about the abutment on the other side." "So," said Mr. Lincoln, "when politicians told me that the Northern and Southern wings of the Democracy could be harmonized, why, I believed them, but I always had my doubts about the abutment on the other side."

Stanton's Impulsiveness.

"WELL," said Mr. Lincoln, "we may have to treat him (Stanton) as they are sometimes obliged to treat a Methodist minister I know of out West. He gets wrought up to so high a pitch of excitement in his prayers and exhortations, that they are obliged to put bricks into his pockets to keep him down. We may be obliged to serve Stanton the same way, but I guess we'll let him jump awhile first."

The "little story" to malcontents, who wished further changes in his Cabinet.

MR. LINCOLN on hearing several of these through with their complaints, with his peculiar smile, said, "Gentlemen, the case reminds me of a story of an old friend of mine out in Illinois. His homestead was much infested with those little black and white animals that we needn't call by name, and, after losing his patience with them he determined to sally out and inflict upon them a general slaughter. He took his gun, clubs and dogs, and at it he went, but stopped after killing one and returned home when his neighbors asked him why he had not fulfiled his threat of killing all there were on his place, he replied that his experience with the one he had killed was such that he thought he had better stop where he was."

His "little story" to Admiral Goldsborough.

IN a conversation with Major-General Garfield, he said: "By the way, Garfield, do you know that Chase, Stanton, General Wool and I had a campaign of our own? We went down to Fortress Monroe in Chase's revenue cutter, and consulted with Admiral Goldsborough on the feasibility of taking Norfolk by landing on the north shore and making a march of eight miles. The Admiral said there was no landing on that shore, and we should have to double the cape, and approach the place from the south side, which would be a very long journey, and a difficult one. I asked him if he had ever tried to find a landing, and he replied that he had not. I then told him a story of a fellow in Illinois who had studied law, but had never tried a case. He was sued, and, not having confidence in his ability to manage his own case, employed a lawyer to manage it for him. He had only a confused idea of the meaning of law terms, but was anxious to make a display of learning, and, on the trial, constantly made suggestions to his lawyer, who paid but little attention to him. At last, finding that his lawyer was not handling the opposing counsel very well, he lost all his patience ; and, springing to his feet, cried out, ' Why don't you go at him with a *capias* or a *surre-butter* or *nudem-puctum* ? 'Now, Admiral,' said I, 'if you don't know that there is no landing on the north shore, I want you to find out.'"

Doing all the Swearing for the Regiment.

HERE is a little story told by General Fisk that Mr. Lincoln relished very much, and often repeated. The General had begun his military life as a colonel; and, when he raised his regiment in Wisconsin, he proposed to his men that he should do all the swearing of the regiment. They assented ; and for months no instance was known of the violation of the promise. The Colonel had a teamster named John Todd, who, as the roads were not always the best, had some difficulty in commanding his temper and his tongue. John happened to be driving a mule-team through a series of mud-pools a little worse than usual, when, unable to restrain himself any longer, he burst forth in a volly of energetic oaths. The colonel took notice of the offense, and brought John to an account, "John," said he, "didn't you promise to let me do all the swearing of the regiment ?" "Yes, I did, Colonel," he replied, "but the fact was the swearing had to be done then, or not at all, and you weren't there to do it."

About Making Brigadier-Generals.

A PERSON who wishes to be commissioned as Brigadier told Mr. Lincoln in a sarcastic tone, "I see there's no va-cancies among the Brigadiers, from the fact that so many colonels are commanding brigades."

"My friend, "said Mr. Lincoln, "let me tell you something about that. You are a farmer I believe ; if not, you will understand me. Suppose you had a large cattle yard, full of all sorts of cattle—cows, oxen and bulls,—and you kept killing and selling and disposing of your cows and oxen, in one way and another, taking good care of your bulls. By and by you would find out that you had nothing but a yard full of old bulls, good for nothing under heavens. Now it will be just so with the army, if I don't stop making Brigadier-Generals."

Let 'em Wriggle.

"The Wade and Davis matter troubles me but little," Mr. Lincoln said to a friend. "Indeed I feel a good deal about it as the old man did about his cheese when his very smart boy found, by the aid of a microscope, that it was full of maggots. "Oh father!" exclaimed the boy, "how can you eat that stuff? just look in here and see 'em wriggle!" The old man took another mouthful, and, putting his teeth into it, replied grimly; "let 'em wriggle!"

A Hard Hit.

At the conference in Hampton Roads, Mr. Lincoln declared that, in his negotiations for peace, he could not recognize another government inside of the one of which he alone was President.

Mr. Hunter replied that "the recognition of Davis' power to make a treaty was the first indespensible step to peace," and, to illustrate his point, he refered to the correspondence between King Charles the First and his Parliment, as a reliable precedent of a constitutional rule treating with rebels.

"Upon questions of history," replied Lincoln "I must refer you to Seward, for he is posted in such things, and I don't profess to be ; but my only distinct recollection of the matter is that *Charles lost his head.*"

It Did Her So Much Good.

On an other occasion refering to the same he said, "It reminds me of a man in Illinois whose wife occasionally took the broomstick to him. His neighbors remonstrated with the unfortunate husband and told him he was scandalized as a man in allowing her to do this, "O," said he shrugging up his shoulder and at the same time giving a comical look "I don't mind it then it seems to do her a heap of good."

Abraham Lincoln's Duel.

SOMETHING more than a score of years ago, Springfield, the capital of the Prairie State, was the home of a maiden, who was as bright as she was beautiful, and as spirited and witty, as she was graceful and good. If we do not name her, it is because in her place in our heart she is too well hedged around by love and reverence to be brought forth and presented to the profane gaze of the public. As the wife of a senator, whom all good men, and women, too, delight to honor, her conserving and purifying power has since been shown to the world by the influence it has had in helping him keep his life pure and noble.

This maiden, whom we will call Anna, because we must call her something, was the friend and confidant of Miss Todd, the affianced of Mr. Lincoln, who had, not so very many years before this, left off splitting rails, to try what skill he might have in splitting hairs in a lawyer's office in Springfield. Judge Shields was likewise a dweller in the town at this time, and a frequenter of the society in which the two "bright, particular stars," already mentioned, shed their radiance. But his moral character was not altogether immaculate, report said. For this, or some other reason, Anna was not inclined to regard him with favor. Once upon a time, however, circumstances compelled her to accept his escort from an evening party to her father's house. Her spirit was moved with indignation by a trifling incident which occurred on the way, and she determined upon securing revenge.

A day or two afterwards some verses appeared in the literary luminary of the place, the name of which Father Time has, or, at any rate, we have, dropped from the scene. The verses were addressed to Judge S. so obviously, that he who ran could read, though his name did not appear. They were witty and sharp, and though everybody knew at once to whom they referred, everybody did not know who wrote them. Among the unfortunate ones to whom, in this case, ignorance was not bliss, was the distinguished individual to whom they were addressed, who might naturally be supposed to have a more than common interest in having ignorance

supplanted by knowledge, in converting the unknown into the known. He set about the accomplishment of the
desired end, but soon found that the pursuit of knowledge on that line was emphatically following after it under difficulties. He went to the editor, or printer, perhaps the quality was comprised in one person, and, after
the old man in the spelling book, first tried gentle measures, which, not availing, in imitation of the same illus-
trious example, he proceeded to try what virtue there
was in severe ones, which soon brought the editor down,
and he confessed that the verses were handed to him in
the handwriting of Miss Todd. He did not tell him, because he did not know, that she had only copied them
from the manuscript of her friend Anna.

Judge S. ungallantly attacked the supposed writer in a
rejoinder, which appeared in the next issue of the same
paper. Springfield was not so large then but that everybody knew his neighbor's business as well as he did himself, if not a little better. The matter was discussed at
every fireside, and came in with dessert, if not before,
at every dinner table.

It was well known that Miss Todd was betrothed to
Mr. Lincoln, and every principle of law and equity demanded that he should be her defender against all wrong
and injustice. He would be no loyal knight if he should
suffer his lady love to be publicly attacked and he not
come to the rescue. He therefore, took up the cudgel
in her behalf, and the result was a challenge from Judge
Shields to meet him in single combat and undo the
wrong that had been done, by the pleasant operation of
the one shedding the other's blood. Whatever may have
been Mr. Lincoln's feelings about duelling in the abstract,
in this particular case there seemed to be no choice left
him but to accept the challenge. Miss Todd was a Ken-
tuckian. The friends with whom she lived were of the
same ilk. Mr. Lincoln himself had been cradled under
the same sky. The mere semblance of pusillanimity was
something that must be put far from him. He accepted
the challenge, and having the right of choice in regard
to weapons, selected broad swords.

But the laws of Illinois are very stringent in regard to

duelling. That kind of salve for a man's wounded honor was not among the prescriptions contained in its code. Years before this the legislature had declared duelling a capital offense and one unfortunate violator of the statute had died at the hands of the hangman. Thenceforth common men pocketed the offences which the law would not vindicate. The chivalry, when insulted, had to nurse their wrath until they could get into Missouri, or at least to Bloody Island, halfway over the Mississippi.

This was before the railroads with their iron horses and fabulous speed had wakened the echoes in that region. Springfield was a respectable two days' journey from Alton, the nearest accessible point to the Mississippi. As nothing else could be done, these two chivalric defenders of injured innocence collected their swords and other traps and started on a slow coach, with the privilege of having by the way, a nice long time in which to think of the pleasantness of killing or being killed, and what might come thereafter. At last the journey ended, as all things earthly must, and they arrived at Alton.

There were no steam ferry-boats then. The Charons of that day had to find motive power in their own sinewy arms. Everything was favorable to reflection. The time was abundant not only for "sober, second thought," to try its power, but that number had a chance to multiply itself into thousands, and grow soberer all the while. But nothing moved the combatants from their steady purpose. The father of waters was propitious, and they with their swords and a man with a dish to catch the blood and a string to take up an artery, as the case might require. The matter having being noised abroad somewhat in Alton, some persons, blessed with enquiring minds, followed them across the river in order to be in at the death. As the news spread more and more, there came to be quite an excitement in the town among those who remained, and sentinels were posted in commanding positions, and close watch was kept for the party when it should return. In process of time the watchman announced that the boat which had been freighted with the valiant, was coming back, and when it was a third of the way in its passage across the river, sharp eyes detected a man with his cloak wrapped around him lying in the bottom of the flat-boat. The news spread quickly over the town that one of the avengers of nobody knew exactly what, had fallen a victim to his courage ; and womanly eyes were ready to weep at the thought of the havoc that would be made in somebody's heart. But now, as often, the near contradicted the far. When the boat landed it was found that some wag had put in a log, and thrown over it a cloak, so that expectation might not be let down too suddenly from its elevation. The victims who had so bravely prepared themselves for the sacrifice, was both alive and well. Their honor had been healed by other plaster than that of blood. When the danger came within touching distance, their wrath became placable. A friend who had got an inkling of what was on hand, had followed them, and reached the place as Lincoln was clearing away the brush to have a chance for a fair fight, and succeeded, just in the nick of time, in convincing them, as many another man has been convinced, that "discretion is the better part of valor."

To Mr. Lincoln, with his quick sense of the ridiculous, and nice appreciation of humor, the whole thing must have been very laughable in after years, unless, which is possible, it was a little bit mortifying. Whether he ever used the story to illustrate the parturition of mountains and the bringing forth of mice, I do not know. He probably would have done so, had he not himself have been the hero.

Every Man His own Boss.

But one argument in the support of the repeal of the Missouri Compromise is still to come. That argument is "the sacred right of self-government." It seems our distinguished Senator has found great difficulty in getting his antagonists, even in the Senate, to meet him fairly on this argument. Some poet has said, "Fools rush in where angels fear to tread."

At the hazard of being thought one of the fools of this quotation, I meet that argument,—I rush in,—I take that bull by the horns. . . . I say that, that no man is good enough to govern another man *without that other's consent.* I say, this is the leading principle, the sheet-

anchor of American Republicanism. Our Declaration
of Independence says: "That, to secure these rights,
governments are instituted among men, DERIVING THEIR
JUST POWERS FROM THE CONSENT OF THE GOVERNED."
Now, the relation of master and slave is, *pro tanto*, a
total violation of their principle. The master not only
governs the slave without his consent, but he governs
him by a set of rules altogether different from those
which he prescribes for himself. Allow ALL the governed an equal voice in the government; and that, and
that only, is self-government. . . . If it is a sacred right
for the people of Nebraska to take and hold slaves there,
it is equally their sacred right to buy them where they
can buy them cheapest; and that, undoubtedly, will be
on the coast of Africa, provided you will consent not to
hang them for going there to buy them. . . . He (the
African slave-dealer) honestly buys them at the rate of
about a red cotton handkerchief a head. This is very
cheap; and it is a great abridgment of the "*sacred right
of self-government*," to hang men for engaging in this
profitable trade.—*Speech, October,* 1854.

Little "Tad" as Attorney-General.

FOR my own part, if I wanted an agent to procure anything like a pardon from Mr. Lincoln, I should have
unhesitatingly sent a child rather than a grown woman
of any kind. Anything like helplessness appealed to
him strongly, and he was very fond of children at all
times.

To such an extent did he carry this indulgence for
little "Tad" [the President's favorite son] who, by the
way, was a very intelligent and affectionate boy, that he
allowed him free access to his business office at all hours
and under almost any circumstances; and I well remember the dignified expression of disapprobation with which
a testy old Senator declared his opinion that "that boy
was becoming decidedly more numerous than popular."

Tad had the same weakness for unlucky brutes which
his father had for unfortunate men, and always had
under his protection. one or more ill-conditioned curs of
low degree, famished appearance and unimaginable ex-

traction. Somehow they never stayed long, and I do
not know whether or not they fattened as well as others
at the "public crib."

Nor were there wanting biped petitioners who were
quick to seize upon what seemed so vulnerable a point
as Mr. Lincoln's affection for his boy, and attempt to
bring themselves to the favorable notice of the all powerful President by the assiduty with which they cultivated his little pet. Of course they succeeded with Tad,
for a boy's heart is easily fished for, and there were a
few of the earlier approaches on this line which were
tolerably successful; but only a very few found their
way to his knee or table before Mr. Lincoln saw the
point, and "Tad's clients" became more a matter for
joke than anything else. Otherwise, as a general rule,
it was not apt to be to any man's advantage to have his
case pressed by a member of the President's family.

Cool.

But you will not abide the election of a Republican
President. In that supposed event, you say, you will
destroy the Union; and then, you say, the great crime
of having destroyed it will be upon us.

That is cool. A highwayman holds a pistol to my ear,
and mutters through his teeth, "Stand and deliver, or I
shall kill you; and then you will be a murderer!" To
be sure, what the robber demanded of me—my money—
was my own, and I had a clear right to keep it: but it
was no more my own than my vote is my own; and the
threat of death to me, to extort my money, and the
threat of destruction to the Union, to extort my vote,
can scarcely be distinguished in principle.—*Speech, February,* 1860.

The Mortgaged Widow.

A widow woman from Michigan, was unable to meet
a mortgage of a few hundred dollars on her little home,
and she determined to get it from the President. In
her simple mind she had no doubt of his boundless
wealth, or that when once he heard her story he would
pay off the mortgage. So she raised some money among
her neighbors by subscription, and started for Washing-

ton, traveling by all sorts of conveyances, and of course taking the longest road, and bringing her four little children with her. How she did it is a mystery only to be solved by Him who feeds the young ravens, but she actually reached the capital with more money than when she started, and fell into kind and charitable hands when she got there. Of course she saw Mr. Lincoln, and he listened to her story and read her letters with a half humorous, half vexed expression that was irresistible.

He did not say much, only muttering "children and fools, you know," but put his name on the subscription papers for a moderate sum. The subscription so started rapidly swelled to the desired amount, and the poor woman was ticketed homeward over the Government routes, puzzled and yet satisfied. She had spent more money, going and coming, than the whole of debt twice over. Such is wisdom.

Don't Swap Horses while Crossing the River.

I AM not insensible at all to the personal compliment there is in this; and yet I do not allow myself to believe, that any but a small portion of it is to be appropriated as a personal compliment. . . . The part I am entitled to appropriate as a compliment is only that part which I may lay hold of as being the opinion of the Convention and the League, that I am not entirely unworthy to be intrusted with the place which I have occupied for the last three years. But I do not allow myself to suppose, that either the Convention or the League have concluded to decide that I am either the greatest or best man in America; but rather they have concluded, *that it is not best to swap horses while crossing the river;* and have further concluded, *that I am not so poor a horse, that they might not make a botch of it in trying to swap.*—*Speech, June,* 1864.

Which Line He Fights On.

IT is a pertinent question, often asked in the mind privately, and from one to the other, When is the war to end? Surely I feel as deep an interest in this question as any other can; but I do not wish to name a day, a month, or a year, when it is to end. . . . . We accepted this war for an object,—a worthy object; and the war will end when that object is attained. Under God, I hope it never will end until that time. Speaking of the present campaign, General Grant is reported to have said, "I am going through on this line, if it takes all summer." This war has taken three years; it was begun, or accepted, upon the line of restoring the national authority over the whole national domain ; and for the American people, as far as my knowledge enables me to speak, I say, we are going through on *this line*, if it takes three years more.—*Speech, June*, 1864.

He Counts for Sambo.

THE following incident, as related by the Washington correspondent of the "Chicago Tribune," is a touching instance of his genuine goodness of heart, combined with the native simplicity of a country gentleman :—

" I dropped in upon Mr. Lincoln on Monday last, and found him busily engaged in counting greenbacks. 'This, sir,' said he, 'is something out of my usual line ; but a President of the United States has a multiplicity of duties not specified in the Constitution, or Acts of Congress ; this is one of them. This money belongs to a poor negro, who is a porter in one of the departments (the Treasury), and who is at present very sick with the small-pox. He is now in the hospital, and could not draw his pay, because he could not sign his name. 'I have been at considerable trouble to overcome the difficulty, and get it for him ; and have at length succeeded in cutting red tape, as you newspaper-men say. I am now dividing the money, and putting by a portion, labelled in an envelope with my own hands, according to his wish.' "

"Old Abe!"

SPEAKING of a certain class of applicants for office, reminds Secretary S. of a fat and ruddy individual, in a swallow-tailed coat, who entered his office one morning with an expression of the most beaming, gushing, greasy and cordial familiarity, and asked "if Old Abe was in ?"

" Whom, sir ?"

"Why, Old Abe? I want to see him a few mimutes. How is the old fellow, anyway ?"

"Really, sir, I cannot imagine of whom you can be

inquiring, unless, indeed, by any accident you are trying
to speak of the President of the United States. If so,
he is in, but you can't see him to-day.

"Not see Old Abe! Why not?"

It required several unsatisfactory remarks to explain
matters to him. I wonder if some people do imagine it
a smart thing to address even letters to public men by
their nick-names; and, if so, how soon they get their
answers on an average.

Pop-Guns, etc.

ONE universal idea seemed to be that if any given gun,
cannon, ship, armor or all-killing or all-saving apparatus
chanced to take the eye of the President, it must thereupon speedily be adopted for army use and forced into a
grand success by Executive authority. It was in vain
that Mr. Lincoln systematically discouraged this notion,
and never went further, even with inventions that pleased
him most, than to order an examination and trial by the
proper professional authorities. Every inventor posted
straight to the White House with his "working model."
Mr. Lincoln had very good mechanical ability, and quick
appreciation of what was practical in any proposed improvement. Here, as elsewhere, his strong common
sense came in play, to the great discomfiture of many a
shallow quack and mechanical enthusiast. It was a common thing for the makers of the new rifles, shells.
armor-vests, gunboats, breech-loading cannon, and the
multitudinous nameless contrivances which came into
being in the heat and excitement of the times by a
species of spontaneous generation, either to invite him
to witness a trial or to send him a specimen—the latter
being frequently intended as a "presentation copy."
On the grounds near the Potomac, south of the White
House, was a huge pile of old lumber, not to be damaged
by balls, and a good many mornings I, says his Private
Secretary, have been out there with the President, by
previous appointment, to try such rifles as were sent in.
There was no danger of hitting any one, and the President, who was a very good shot, enjoyed the relaxation
very much. One morning early we were having a good
time—he with his favorite "Spencer," and I with

a villainous kicking nondescript, with a sort of patent back-action breech, that left my shoulder black and blue—when a squad from some regiment which had just been put on guard in that locality pounced on us for what seemed to them a manifest disobedience of all "regulations." I heard the shout of the officer in command and saw them coming, but as the President was busy drawing a very particular bead—for I had been beating him a little—I said nothing until down they came. In response to a decidedly unceremonious hail, the President, in some astonishment, drew back from his stooping posture, and turned upon them the full length six feet four of their beloved "Commanner-in-Chief." They stood and looked one moment, and then fairly ran away, leaving his Excellency laughing heartily at their needless discomfiture. He only remarked : "Well, they might have stayed and seen the shooting."

The Presidental Umbrella.

EDWARD—the venerable messenger at the door of the President's room—for four administrations doorkeeper of the White House, was an inexhaustible well of incident and anecdote concerning the old worthies and unworthies. An undersized, neatly dressed, polite, comical old man, with a world of genuine Irish wit in his white head. He it was who went with Fillmore to look at a carriage which the necessities of some Southern magnate had thrown upon the market.

"Well, Edward," said the President, "and how will it do for the President of the United States to buy a second-hand carriage?"

"And sure, yer Excellency, and ye're only a second-hand President, ye know!"

Mr. Fillmore took the joke, but not the carriage. This anecdote was told me by Mr. Lincoln, and was called up by the following : One dark and rainy evening we had got as far as the door, on our way to Gen. McClellan's headquarters, without an umbrella, and Edward was sent back after one, the President telling him whereabouts he might find it. In a few minutes he came back, announcing a fruitless search, and adding,

"Sure, yer Excellency, and the owner must have come for it!"

The President laughed heartily, and Edward found us another umbrella.

The Lost " Little Fat Man."

SOME people attended "levees," as they were called, with the dim idea that they were about to make the acquaintance of the President and his wife, and prepared themselves for a quiet little chat, with stores of questions about this and advice about that for Father Abraham. Others, not expecting much time to themselves, would prepare patriotic little speeches, which they would launch with sudden fervor and wonderfully rapid utterance at the head of the President. There was a little wee bit of a fat man, half smothered in the crowd, stretching out a hand through a chink in the procession, as if he was drowning, and while the laughing President shook him almost convulsively thereby, the persistent little orator under difficulties, wheezed out some choked sentences about freedom, glory, emancipation, etc. When Mr. Lincoln let go of him he disappeared.

Smokers Smoked Out.

IN the latter part of the war a formal guard was kept, says his Private Secretary, both at the White House and when the President was at the Soldiers' Home. This guard were proud of their duty, and sometimes exerted a degree of zeal that might have been dispensed with. At one time, after several wooden buildings, containing army stores, etc., had been destroyed by fire, a general order was issued by the Commander of the District, forbidding any one to approach any of the public buildings with a lighted cigar. Although the intent of the order was clear enough, the officer in command of the President's Guard decided that it applied to the Executive Mansion and grounds. In consequence, that evening, as I approached the gate, puffing away at my customary after-dinner Havana, I was compelled, by the rifleman on duty, to pitch my luxury into the gutter, in spite of sundry grumbling expostulations. There was, however, a mounted man also on guard, and before I had proceeded many steps he shouted, "Hey! Mr. Secretary, won't you just come here a moment?" and as I approached him, "that wooden-headed cuss has got off a couple of good jokes since he came on, if he only knew it, and I wish you would tell them to Mr. Lincoln. I'll bet he'll laugh well. You see he hadn't been there five minutes, with his head full of his new order, when along comes old Seward, and you know he's always a smokin'. Well, he didn't want to throw his cigar away, a bit, but he was good natured about it, and said something about people having to give up a good many things on account of the war, and he went on. Then, in a minute or so, up comes Ben. Butler, in full military fig, and he was smokin' too. 'You musht put out dat cigar,' says guardy, for he's Dutch as ——. 'Are those your orders, sir?' says Butler, drawing himself up, and trying to look at the fellow with both eyes. 'Well, sir, orders are orders, and they must be obeyed!' And so the General threw his cigar over the fence. It's a humbug, you know, but then it's fun to see cocks like them obeying orders."

The thing was funny, and quite reconciled me to my loss. When I related it to Mr. Lincoln he laughed heartily. "What! did Seward throw his cigar away?"

"Yes, sir."

"And Ben. Butler too?"

"Yes, with appropriate remarks."

"Well, it's a very good joke, but I guess it has gone far enough."

So the zealous captain of the guard was sent for and the prohibition removed, to the great comfort of all the smokers. It was said that the boys caught Mr. Stanton himself before they lifted the embargo, but I do not know how truly.

The 2d Inaugural Address,

4TH OF MARCH, 1865.

FELLOW-COUNTRYMEN—At this second appearing to take the oath of the Presidential office, there is less occasion for an extended address than there was at the first. Then a statement somewhat in detail of a course to be pursued seemed very fitting and proper. Now, at

the expiration of four years, during which public declara-
tions have constantly been called forth on every point
and phase of the great contest which still absorbs the
attention and engrosses the energies of the nation, little
that is new could be presented.

The progress of our arms, upon which all else chiefly
depends, is as well known to the public as to myself;
and it is, I trust, reasonably satisfactory and encouraging
to all. With high hope for the future, no prediction in
regard to it is ventured. On the occasion corresponding
to this, four years ago, all thoughts were anxiously di-
rected to an impending civil war. All dreaded it, all
sought to avoid it. While the inaugural address was
being delivered from this place, devoted altogether to
saving the Union without war, insurgent agents were in
the city, seeking to destroy it without war—seeking to
dissolve the Union and divide the effects by negotiation.

Both parties deprecated war; but one of them would
make war rather than let the nation survive, and the
other would accept war rather than let it perish : and the
war came.

One-eighth of the whole population were colored
slaves, not distributed generally over the Union, but
located in the southern part of it. These slaves consti-
tuted a peculiar and powerful interest. All knew that
this interest was somehow the cause of the war. To
strengthen, perpetuate, and extend this interest was the
object for which the insurgents would rend the Union
by war, while Government claimed no right to do more
than to restrict the territorial enlargement of it. Neither
party expected the magnitude or the duration which it
has already attained. Neither anticipated that the cause
of the conflict might cease, even before the conflict
itself should cease. Each looked for an easier triumph,
and a result less fundamental and astounding. Both
read the same Bible and pray to the same God, and each
invokes his aid against the other. It may seem strange
that any man should dare to ask a just God's assistance
in wringing his bread from the sweat of other men's
faces. But let us judge not, that we be not judged. The
prayer of both should not be answered. That of neither

has been answered fully.   The Almighty has his own
purposes.   "Woe unto the world because of offences,
for it must needs be that offences come; but woe to that
man by whom the offence cometh."   If we shall suppose
that American slavery is one of these offences, which, in
the providence of God, must needs come, but which,
having continued through his appointed time, he now
wills to remove, and that he gives to both North and
South this terrible war as the woe due to those by whom
the offence came, shall we discern therein any departure
from those divine attributes which the believers in a living God always ascribe to him ?

Fondly do we hope, fervently do we pray, that this
mighty scourge of war may speedily pass away.   Yet if
God wills that it continue until all the wealth piled by the
bondman's two hundred and fifty years of unrequited
toil shall be sunk, and until every drop of blood drawn
with the lash shall be paid by another drawn with the
sword; as was said three thousand years ago, so still it
must be said, that the judgments of the Lord are true
and righteous altogether.

With malice towards none, with charity for all, with
firmness in the right, as God gives us to see the right, let
us strive on to finish the work we are in; to bind up the
nation's wound; to care for him who shall have borne
the battle, and for his widow and his orphans; to do all
which may achieve and cherish a just and lasting peace
among ourselves, and with all nations.

Lincoln for President, Doctor!

My first view of Mr. Lincoln as the great man he really
was happened in this wise.   Some nine months before
the meeting of the Chicago Republican Convention in
1860, my partner and I began to discuss the subject,
"Whose name shall we hang out as our candidate?"   It
was still full early in the season, and we were in no hurry
for a decision.   The writer of the above, Mr. Stoddard,
goes on to state :

Early one morning, just after I had finished my break-
fast, I strolled into the office of the hotel where I
boarded, for a chat with some one before going to work.
The room was empty when I entered, but in a moment

the door opened and Mr. Lincoln came in. He seated himself quietly by the fire and took off his hat, which was packed full of letters just taken from the Post-Office. I was about to speak to him, as usual, when I was arrested by something thoughtful and abstracted in his manner, and, as I always had a "strong weakness" for taking observations of remarkable men, I kept my seat in silence. He opened letter after letter, burning some and glancing hastily over others, until he reached one somewhat longer than common, which seemed to affect him profoundly. He was evidently thinking, and thinking deeply; and so few men know by experience what genuine hard thinking is, that I fear that this will hardly convey my meaning.

Leaning forward, with his hands folded across his knee, he gazed abstractedly into the fire, his rugged face gradually lighting up with vivid and changing expressions until it was almost transfigured.

I felt, without knowing how or why, that the gaunt form before me was that of no ordinary man. I had seen, and, as it were, accidentally looked into (through his face) one of the great ones of history. Long as I knew him afterwards, I never saw so much of him again.

Without disturbing him, I quietly stole from the room and hurried to my office.

"Doctor, I have made up mind whom we are going to support for the next Presidency."

"Well, who is it?"

"Abraham Lincoln, of Illinois!"

"What! Old Abe? Nonsense!"

"No nonsense about it, I tell you. He is our man, for certain."

"Pshaw! every one likes him well enough, but we never could get him nominated. For Vice President now, and because we are Illinoisans—"

"Lincoln for President, Doctor, and nobody else. My mind is made up."

And as I generally had my own way, after a brief trip to Springfield to open communication with his friends, etc., the name of Abraham Lincoln blazed in broad letters at our editorial masthead. We were, as far as

known, the first in the field, and it had an important
result for me, of which, at that time, I never dreamed;
it drew Mr. Lincoln's attention to me personally, and
procured for me, the opportunity I afterwards had, in
his own household, of learning a still more profound
reverence for the great man I had seen in the light of
the fire that chilly prairie morning.

"In Love."

LYING before me upon my study-table, says Mr. F. B.
Carpenter in a very interesting series of "Unpublished
Incidents and Anecdotes of Abraham Lincoln," is a plain
brown leather-bound book, bearing the marks both of
age and use. The title-page, in old-fashioned leather,
contains the words,

"THE WORKS OF LORD BYRON.
Philadelphia : Griggs & Elliott.
1838."

Upon the fly-leaf is written in ink,

"A. LINCOLN,
Presented by his friend, N. W. Edwards."

This is in Mr. Lincoln's hand-writing. Upon the page
facing this are two columns of figures in pencil, which
look like election returns, with their footing carefully
computed—also in Mr. Lincoln's hand. Underneath
there is an inscription by the Hon. Wm. H. Herndon,
of Springfield, Ill., who requests, in characteristic phrase,
that "this book" may be kept in the possession of the
friend to whom he dedicates it, "for the *forever* of
books."

A letter accompanied the gift, in which Mr. Herndon
states that "this book was given to Mr. Lincoln by his
brother-in-law, N. W. Edwards, in 1839 or 40;" that
"Mr. Lincoln read it year in and year out, till Shakespeare and Euclid swallowed up all other books." Several
other old volumes accompanied its presentation by Mr.
Lincoln to Mr. Herndon—"Goldsmith, Locke, Gibbon,"
in strange company with "Patent Office Reports,"
"Congressional Globes," etc., etc.

A new phase in Mr. Lincoln's character has lately been
opened in the revelation of his early attachment to a
young lady of New Salem, whose death soon after their
engagement threw him into profound melancholy, chang-

ing the whole course of his after life. The "Byron" before me came into his hands within a few years of this event. It bears no marks of pen or pencil other than those described; but upon turning its pages the curious observer is arrested by one folded leaf—one only, in all the book. The page is discolored, and the fold of the leaf seems as old as the book itself—it is firmly, solidly pressed together like a withered flower. The eye runs down the page, and is stopped by *two verses*, entitled

"WRITTEN AT ATHENS, JANUARY 16th, 1810.

"The spell is broke, the charm is flown,
Thus is it with life's fitful fever;
We madly smile when we should groan,
Delirium is our best deceiver.

" Each lucid interval of thought
Recalls the woes of Nature's charter,
And he that acts as wise men ought
But lives, as saints have died, a martyr."

Were these lines to Abraham Lincoln, in 1839, simply co-incident with his thought at this period of his life, or were they a *prophecy?*

"Ploughing Around."

THE enlistment of negroes in the Eastern Department of the army commenced under General Schenck's command, in Maryland, and contemplated at first the enlistment only of the free blacks. Much trouble was occasioned, however, from the fact that it was often impossible to tell whether the "recruits" presenting themselves were free or not; masters frequently coming forward and claiming parties who had enlisted. General Schenck at length went to Washington to ascertain what policy the Administration proposed to pursue in the matter. He stated his case to the President, explaining his difficulties, and asked for instructions. Mr. Lincoln replied that he had no special instructions to give; the condition of things at that juncture was such that it seemed best to have no definite policy on the subject.— Commanders of the departments must act according to their best judgment. "You see, Schenck," continued Mr. Lincoln, "we are like an old acquaintance of mine who settled on a piece of '*galled*' prairie. It was a terrible rough place to clear up; but after a while he got a

few things growing—here and there a patch of corn, a
few hills of beans, and so on. One day a stranger stopped
to look at his place, and wanted to know how he managed
to cultivate so rough a spot. 'Well,' was the reply,
'some of it *is* pretty tough. The smaller stumps I can
generally root out or burn out ; but now and then there
is an old settler that bothers me, and there is no other
way but to plough around it.' "Now, Schenck," Mr.
Lincoln concluded, "at such a time as this, troublesome
cases are constantly coming up, and the only way to get
along at all is to plough around them."

Mr. Lincoln's Waste Basket.

AGAIN and again, says the President's Confidential
officer, have I experienced the liveliest amusement in
having local politicians and others boast of the effect
their advice has evidently had upon the mind of the
President, and describe the course which they had
marked out for his future action. More than one has
asked me if I had ever heard Mr. Lincoln speak of his
letters, and if such and such a one was not read in Cabinet council. Dante should have seen my willow basket
before he completed his list of limbos. Its edge was
truly a bourne from which no traveler returned.

One day a well-dressed gentleman—a judge, or something of the kind, at home—sat in my room looking on
at the performance of my morning job of destruction,
twisting uneasily in his chair, and changing from red to
pale with indignation, until he could contain his gathered wrath no longer. He had evidently indulged in
letter-writing himself.

"Was that the way in which I dared to serve the President's correspondence ? Was this the manner in which
the people were prevented from reaching Mr. Lincoln ?
He would complain of me to my master at once ! Teach
me a thing or two about my duties ! See if this was to
be allowed ! A mere boy in such an important place as
that !" And so on for some moments, until I looked
up and requested him to be still for a moment, while I
read him a few of the precious documents I was des-
troying.

Of course, I made judicious selections to suit the occasion, for he was evidently intensely respectable and patriotic. I began with an epistle full of vulgar abuse that "riled" the old gentleman fearfully. Next I put in a proclamation "written in blood," and signed by the "Angel Gabriel;" and wound up with a horrible thing from an obscene, idiotic lunatic—a regular correspondent. The last was too much for him, and he begged me to stop. It was, indeed, sickening enough. I told him that if he insisted on the President's giving his time to such things he must take them in himself, as really I was forbidden to do so. The old gentleman, however, thought better of me by that time, and leaned back in his chair to moralize on the total depravity of human nature.

Mere " Scrubs."

THE day after the issue of the Emancipation Proclamation Senator Wade called upon the President to congratulate him. He was met by Mr. Lincoln, asking if he remembered the fable illustration of "the attempt to wash the blackamoor *white*," and the result—the death of the *black*. "And," continued Mr. Lincoln, "I fear in this case that between the North and the South the chances are that the poor *negro* will get *scrubbed* to *death.*"

More Whiskey

MR. LINCOLN was a man of genius—a man of powerful instincts and keen intuitions—rather than of close and accurate reasoning powers. In the latter, though his natural abilities were great, he yet at times showed the lack of early systematic training. Perhaps this was a loss, but I incline to the opposite opinion. His perceptions guided him well through labyrinths where logic would have been bewildered. His personal attachments were strong, and may at times have blinded him to faults of character in others which would otherwise have met with his earnest condemnation—though he never committed the absurdity of expecting perfection from his fellow men. His personal habits were of the simplest kind, and there was not a particle of fuss and feathers in his composition. He was not slovenly, but seldom knew or cared whether or not he was well dressed. He used neither tobacco nor intoxicating liquors in any form, though not disposed to quarrel with those who chose to do so. Indeed, once, when a delegation of Grant's enemies (he was then commanding in the West) accused the General of intemperance, he begged them to tell him where Grant got his whiskey, as he would like to purchase a few barrels for some of the Eastern Generals, "if that was what made him behave as he did."

The Pennsylvania Raid.

At the time of the first raid of Lee's army into Maryland and Pennsylvania, much alarm was felt in Philadelphia, lest that city might fall into their hands. A gentleman on his way to Washington, witnessing the excitement in Philadelphia, expected to find Washington also in a ferment. On the contrary, the Capital was as quiet as though "raids" were unknown. Reporting the alarm felt in Philadelphia to Mr. Lincoln, the gentleman expressed his surprise at the absence of excitement in Washington.

"When I was studying law," Mr. Lincoln replied, half abstractedly, "I boarded with a Mr.——. One night I went to bed as usual, and was awakened in the middle of the night by my landlord, who stood by the side of my bed, with nothing on but his shirt, trembling with fright. 'Lincoln,' said he, 'get up! The world is coming to an end!' I jumped out of bed, and ran to a window. And, sure enough, it seemed as though the man was right; all the stars in heaven appeared to be falling. I looked on for some time, expecting a crash; but none came. Finally, I thought I would look for my familiar constellations—the 'Hen and Chickens,' the 'Sow and Pigs,' and 'Ellen Carter.' They were in their old places, shining as serenely as though shooting stars had never been heard of. I watched them awhile; and seeing them firm and steady as ever, I made up my mind that it was not going to be much of a *shower* after all; so I went to bed again. And I think this raid will turn out much the same way."

The President and the Players.

So much has been said about Mr. Lincoln's theatre going that a great many people have imbibed the idea that his tastes were dramatic; but this was not so. With the exception of a few of Shakespeare's plays, it is not believed that he ever read a play in his life.

He was heard to say that there were several of even Shakespeare's dramas at which he had hardly ever looked. "Macbeth" was certainly one of his prime favorities, and he went one night to see Charlotte Cushman as Lady Mabeth. It was, of course, a grand impersonation, but it was impossible to get Mr. Lincoln to make many comments upon it. He seemed to have a poor opinion of his own powers as a dramatic critic. Another of his favorites was "Othello," and he eagerly embraced the opportunity of seeing it when Davenport and Wallack brought it out in Washington. Everbody who was present must have been struck with the keen interest with which he followed the development of Iago's subtle treachery. One would have thought that such a character would have had few points of attraction for a man to whose own nature all its peculiar traits were so utterly foreign. Perhaps he was fascinated by that very contrast.

He did not lose a word or a motion of the actor, who played his part exceedingly well, and conversed between the acts with, for him, a very near approach to excitement. He seemed to be studying what sort of soul a born traitor might have. His strong love of humor made Falstaff a great favorite with him, and he expressed a great desire to see Hackett in that character. The correspondence between that gentleman and Mr. Lincoln has already been published. He expressed himself greatly pleased with the representation, and went more than once during Hackett's engagement. One who was with him the first night, expected to see him give himself up to the merriment of the hour. To the observer's surprise, however, he appeared even gloomy, although intent upon the play, and it was only a few times during the whole performance that he went so far as to laugh at all, and then not heartily. He seemed for once to be studying the character and its rendering critically, as if to ascertain the correctness of his own conception as compared with that of the professional artist. He afterwards received a call from Mr. Hackett,

and conversed freely, frankly acknowledging his want of
accquaintance with dramatic subjects. Had his early
education been of a sort to develope more perfectly his
literary tastes, his keen insight into human nature, and
his appreciation of humorous and other eccentricities of
character, would have enabled him to have derived the
highest degree of enjoyment from the creations of the
great masters. As it was, he probably understood
Shakespeare, so far as he had read him, far better than
many men who set themselves up for critical authorities.
He himself deserves to be depicted by some pen not less
graphic than the immortal bard's.

A Black Man's Note.

MR. HUNTINGTON, cashier of the First National Bank
of Washington, meeting an old friend of Mr. Lincoln's
one morning, remarked, "That President of yours is the
oddest man alive. Why, he endorses notes for niggers!"
It seems that some time before a colored man finding
himself in danger of losing his house for the want of $150,
went to Mr. Lincoln and told his story. The result was
that the man made a two months' note, and Mr. Lincoln
endorsed it. The note was discounted by some one, and
found its way into Huntington's bank for collection.
Upon its maturity the colored man failed to respond.—
Instead of serving the customary notice of protest upon
the endorser, the cashier took the note in person to Mr.
Lincoln, who at once offered to pay it. Mr. Huntington
said : "Mr. President, you have tried to help a fellow-
mortal along. I am not willing that you should suffer
this entire loss ; we will divide it between us," and the
affair was thus settled.

"Model" Men.

SPEAKING of Mr. Lincoln and his guns puts his Secretary in mind of the balloon men. Mr. Lincoln himself
had for years been decidely interested in the science of
ærostation (is that the right word?), and I have a sus-
picion that at some time or other he had meddled with it
practically in a small way. When the army began to
employ balloons for military reconnoissances, a host of
ingenious fellows all over the country turned their attention to the art of ærial navigation, and, as a matter of

course, every man of them was sure that he had the right machine, if he could only get Government to build one of sufficient size to prove it.

It would, indeed, have required a big balloon to have proved the value of some of the inventions whose "drawings and specifications," often accompanied by a small and rude model, from time to time cumbered my table. A good share of these inventors began by a modest request for a few hundred dollars to bring them to Washington. One fellow proposed an iron-clad balloon to carry heavy guns. He succeeded in raising a good laugh, if nothing else.

The most pertinacious of all was a chap who rigged up a sort of wooden model in the basement of the White House—an upright stick with a long arm on a pivot, to which his air-boat was attached. His clock-work and propeller did certainly work until it ran down, and Mr. Lincoln spent an odd hour or so in examining the arrangement. I believe that he voted it "curious but not useful."

Mr. Lincoln as "Deborah."

In May or June, 1862, a delegation of what are known in Pennsylvania as "Progressive Friends" visited Mr. Lincoln, among many others, to urge upon him decisive action upon the slavery question. The delegation was composed of both men and women. In an address delivered upon this occasion Mr. Lincoln was likened to Deborah, the deliverer of Israel; and a quotation was made from his Springfield speech in his campaign with Douglas, with the intimation that he was expected to stand by his anti-slavery principles. The conclusion of the address was followed by a moment's silence. It was evident Mr. Lincoln was somewhat annoyed. Various delegations and many individuals had visited him, urging action in the same direction. He responded in effect that he thought he appreciated to some extent both the position and the difficulties which surrounded him. He referred to his Springfield speech, correcting what he thought an unwarrantable inference from it, and concluded in nearly these words: "It may be, as you have

said, that, like "Deborah," I have been selected by the
Almighty for this great work of Emancipation. In the
event of this being so, it seems to me I can safely be *left*
in the LORD's hands."

The Lincolns Remove to Indiana.

MR. LINCOLN, the father, although a Southerner by
birth and residence, had become early imbued with a
dislike for slavery. With these sentiments he naturally
desired to change his place of residence, and early in
October, 1816, finding a purchaser for his farm, he made
arrangements for the transfer of the property and for
his removal. The price paid by the purchaser was ten
barrels of whiskey, of forty gallons each, valued at two
hundred and eighty dollars, and twenty dollars in
money. Mr. Lincoln was a temperate man, and acceded
to the terms, not because he desired the liquor, but because such transactions in real estate were common, and
recognized as perfectly proper.

The homestead was within a mile or two of the Rolling
Fork river, and as soon as the sale was affected, Mr. Lincoln, with such slight assistance as little Abe could give
him, hewed out a flat-boat, and launching it, filled it with
his household articles and tools and the barrels of whiskey,
and bidding adieu to his son who stood upon the bank,
pushed off, and was soon floating down the stream on his
way to Indiana, to select a new home. His journey down
the Rolling Fork and into the Ohio river was successfully
accomplished, but soon afterwards his boat was unfortu-
nately upset, and its cargo thrown into the water. Some
men standing on the bank witnessed the accident and
saved the boat and its owner, but all the contents of the
craft were lost, except a few carpenter's tools, axes, three
barrels of whiskey and some other articles. He again
started, and proceeded to a well-known ferry on the river,
from whence he was guided into the interior by a resident
of the section of country in which he had landed, and to
whom he had given his boat in payment for his services.
After several days of difficult traveling, much of the time
employed in cutting a road through the forest wide enough
for a team, eighteen miles were accomplished, and Spencer

county, Indiana, was reached. The site for his new home
having been determined upon, Mr. Lincoln left his goods
under the care of a person who lived a few miles distant,
and returning to Kentucky on foot, made preparations to
remove his family. In a few days the party bade farewell
to their old home and slavery, Mrs. Lincoln and her
daughter riding one horse, Abe another, and the father a
third. After a seven days' journey through an uninhab-
ited country, their resting-place at night being a blanket
spread upon the ground, they arrived at the spot selected
for their future residence, and no unnecessary delays were
permitted to interfere with the immediate and successful
clearing of a site for a cabin. An axe was placed in
Abe's hands, and with the additional assistance of a neighbor, in two or three days Mr. Lincoln had a neat house
of about eighteen feet square, the logs composing which
being fastened together in the usual manner by notches,
and the cracks between them filled with mud. It had only
one room, but some slabs laid across logs overhead gave
additional accommodations which were obtained by climb-
ing a rough ladder in one corner. A bed, table and four
stools were then made by the two settlers, father and son,
and the building was ready for occupancy. The loft was
Abe's bedroom, and there night after night for many years,
he who has since occupied the most exalted position in
the gift of the American people, and has dwelt in the
"White House" at Washington, surrounded by all the
comforts that wealth and power can give, slumbered with
one coarse blanket for his mattress and another for his
covering. Although busy during the ensuing winter with
his axe, he did not neglect his reading and spelling, and
also practised frequently with a rifle, the first evidence of
his skill as a marksman being manifested, much to the
delight of his parents, in the killing of a wild turkey,
which had approached too near the cabin. The knowledge
of the use of the rifle was indispensable in the border
settlements at that time, as the greater portion of the
food required for the settlers was procured by it, and the
family which had not among its male members one or
more who could discharge it with accuracy, was very apt
to suffer from a scarcity of provisions.

The Gettysburg Dedication.
(November, 1863.)

"FOURSCORE and seven years ago, our fathers brought
forth upon this continent a new nation, conceived in
Liberty, and dedicated to the proposition that all men
are created equal.   Now we are engaged in a great civil
war, testing whether that nation, or any nation conceived
and so dedicated, can long endure.   We are met on a
great battle-field of that war.   We are met to dedicate a
portion of it as the final resting-place of those who here
gave their lives that that nation might live.   It is altogether fitting and proper that we should do this.

"But, in a larger sense, we cannot dedicate, we cannot
consecrate, we cannot hallow this ground.   The brave
men, living and dead, who struggled here, have conse-
crated it far above our power to add or detract.   The
world will little note, nor long remember, what we say
here ; but it can never forget what they did here.   It is
for us, the living, rather to be dedicated here to the un-
finished work that they have thus far so nobly carried
on.   It is rather for us to be here dedicated to the great
task remaining before us—that from these honored dead
we take increased devotion to the cause for which they
here gave the last full measure of devotion ; that we here
highly resolve that the dead shall not have died in vain ;
that the nation shall, under God, have a new birth of
freedom ; and that the government of the people, by the
people, and for the people, shall not perish from the
earth."

Young "Abe" Learns to Write.

A LITTLE more than a year after removing to Spencer
county, his mother Mrs. Lincoln died, an event which
brought desolation to the hearts of her husband and
children, but to none so much as to Abe.   He had been
a dutiful son, and she one of the most devoted of
mothers, and to her instruction may be traced many of
those traits and characteristics for which he became
remarkable.   Soon after her death, the bereaved lad had
an offer which promised to afford him other employment
during the long monotonous evenings, than the reading

of books, a young man who had removed into the neighborhood having offered to teach him how to write. The opportunity was too fraught with benefit to be rejected, and after a few weeks of practice under the eye of his instructor, and also out of doors with a piece of chalk or charred stick, he was able to write his name, and in less than twelve months could and did write a letter.

His Speeches in the Celebrated Lincoln-Douglas Campaign.

On the second of June, 1858, the Republican State Convention met at Springfield, and nominated Mr. Lincoln as their candidate for the United States Senate. At the close of their proceedings the recipient of their suffrage delivered a speech, which was a forcible exposition of the views and aims of the party of which he was to be the standard-bearer.

The contest which followed was one of the most exciting and remarkable ever witnessed in this country. Mr. Stephen A. Douglas, his opponent, had few superiors as a political debater. His re-election to the Senate would have been equivalent to an indorsement of his acts and views by his State, and at the same time would have promoted his prospects for the Presidential nomination. The Republicans, therefore, determined to defeat him if possible, and to increase the probabilities of success in the movement, selected Mr. Lincoln as the man who was most certain of securing the election. Illinois was stumped throughout its length and breadth by both candidates and their respective advocates, and the people of the entire country watched with interest the struggle. From county to county, township to township, and village to village, the two leaders traveled, frequently in the same car or carriage, and in the presence of immense crowds of men, women and children—for the wives and daughters of the hardy yeomanry were naturally interested—face to face, these two opposing champions argued the important points of their political belief, and contended nobly for the mastery.

During the campaign, Mr. Lincoln paid the following tribute to the Declaration of Independence—

"These communities (the thirteen colonies), by their

representatives in the old Independence Hall, said to the
world of men, 'We hold these truths to be self-evident,
that all men are born equal; that they are endowed by
their Creator with inalienable rights; that among these
are liberty, and the pursuit of happiness.' This was
their majestic interpretation of the economy of the uni-
verse. This was their lofty, and wise, and noble under-
standing of the justice of the Creator to His creatures.
Yes, gentlemen, to His creatures, to the whole great
family of man. In their enlightened belief, nothing
stamped with the Divine image and likeness was sent
into the world to be trodden on, and degraded, and im-
bruted by its fellows. They grasped not only the race
of men then living, but they reached forward and seized
upon the furtherest posterity. They created a beacon to
guide their children and their children's children, and
the countless myriads who should inhabit the earth in
other ages. Wise statesmen as they were, they knew the
tendency of prosperity to breed tyrants, and so they
established these great self-evident truths that when, in
the distant future, some man, some faction, some interest, should set up the doctrine that none but rich
men, or none but white men, or none but Anglo-Saxon
white men, were entitled to life, liberty, and the pursuit
of happiness, their posterity might look up again to the
Declaration of Independence, and take courage to renew
the battle which their fathers began, so that truth, and
justice, and mercy, and all the humane and Christian
virtues might not be extinguished from the land; so that
no man would hereafter dare to limit and circumscribe
the great principles on which the temple of liberty was
being built.

"Now, my countrymen, if you have been taught doc-
trines conflicting with the great landmarks of the Declaration of Independence; if you have listened to suggestions which would take away from its grandeur, and mu-
tilate the fair symmetry of its proportions; if you have
been inclined to believe that all men are not created
equal in those inalienable rights enumerated by our
chart of liberty, let me entreat you to come back—return to the fountain whose waters spring close by the

blood of the Revolution. Think nothing of me, take no thought for the political fate of any man whomsoever, but come back to the truths that are in the Declaration of Independence.

"You may do anything with me you choose, if you will but heed these sacred principles. You may not only defeat me for the Senate, but you may take me and put me to death. While pretending no indifference to earthly honors, I *do claim* to be actuated in this contest by something higher than an anxiety for office. I charge you to drop every paltry and insignificant thought for any man's success. It is nothing; I am nothing ; Judge Douglas is nothing. *But do not deseroy that immortal emblem of humanity—the Declaratton of American Independence.*"

His Skill as a Rail-Splitter.

WHEN he was mentioned prominently for the Presidency, at a meeting of the Illinois State Republican Convention, where he was present as a spectator, a veteran Democrat of Macon county brought in and presented to the Convention two old fence rails, gayly decorated with flags and ribbons, and upon which the following words were inscribed :

ABRAHAM LINCOLN,

THE RAIL CANDIDATE

FOR PRESIDENT IN 1860.

Two rails from a lot of 3,000 made in 1830, by
Thos. Hanks and Abe Lincoln —whose
father was the first pioneer
of Macon county.

The event occasioned the most unbounded enthusiasm, and for several minutes the most deafening applause resounded through the building. Mr. Lincoln was vociferously called for, and arising from his seat, modestly acknowledged that he had split rails some thirty years previous in Macon county, and he was informed that those before him were a small portion of the product of his labor with the axe.

A Few More.

IT may be convenient to add to the foregoing the following :—

In 1849, he left Congress. In 1856, he received one hundred and two votes, in the Republican Convention, as a candidate for Vice-President, to run with Mr. Fremont. The Republicans of Illinois named him at the head of their electoral ticket, which did not succeed. In 1858, when a senator was to be elected, he and Mr. Douglas canvassed the State together, in that discussion, which gained a national celebrity, and from which we have made several extracts.

On the 16th May, 1860, in the last year of Mr. James Buchanan's career, the Republican National Convention met at Chicago. On the third ballot, Mr. Lincoln was named its candidate for the Presidency. The following incident is preserved of the announcement of the news to him. Such incidents go far towards illustrating the traits of character which endeared him so truly where he was best known.

The superintendent of the Telegraph Company wrote on a scrap of paper,—"Mr. Lincoln : You are nominated on the third ballot ;" and a boy ran with the message to Mr. Lincoln. He looked at it in silence, amid the shouts of those around him ; then, rising and putting it in his pocket, he said quietly, "There's a little woman down at our house would like to hear this. I'll go down, and tell her."

On the 6th of November, 1860, he was elected President. The popular vote gave—

Lincoln	1,866,452
Douglas	1,375,157
Bell	590,631
Breckinridge	847,953

Mr. Lincoln, and Mr. Hamlin, the Vice-President, received 180 electoral votes. Mr. Bell received 39 ; Mr. Douglas received 12 ; Mr. Breckinridge received 72.

On his journey to Washington, in February, 1861, he was received everywhere with enthusiasm. The rebellion had already broken out, and the country had to look to him as its Chief Magistrate. It is in this journey that the following anecdotes find place :—

At Northeast Station, he took occasion to say, that,

during the campaign, he had received a letter from a young girl of the place, in which he was kindly ad-monished to do certain things; and, among others, to let his whiskers grow; and, as he had acted upon that piece of advice, he would now be glad to welcome his fair correspondent, if she was among the crowd. In response to the call, a lassie made her way through the crowd, was helped to the platform, and was kissed by the President.

At Utica he said, " I appear before you that I may see you, and that you may see me; and I am willing to ad-mit, that, so far as the ladies are concerned, I have the best of the bargain; though I wish it to be understood, that I do not make the same acknowledgment concerning the men."

At Hudson he said, " I see you have provided a plat-form; but I shall have to decline standing on it. I had to decline standing on some very handsome platforms prepared for me yesterday. But I say to you, as I said to them, you must not on this account draw the infer-ence, that I have any intention to desert any platform I have a legitimate right to stand on."

At Philadelphia, information was received which made it certain that even then a plot was laid against his life. This caution probably had reached him, when, at a flag-raising on Independence Hall, Philadelphia, he used these remarkable words :—

" I have often inquired of myself, what great principle or idea it was that kept this confederacy so long together. It was something in the Declaration of Independence, giving liberty, not only to the people of this country, but hope to the world for all future time. It was that which gave promise, that, in due time, the weights should be lifted from the shoulders of all men, and that all should have an equal chance. . . . Now, my friends, can this country be saved upon this basis ? If it can, I will con-sider myself one of the happiest men in the world, if I can help to save it. But, if this country cannot be saved without giving up that principle, I was about to say, I would rather be assassinated upon the spot than to sur-render it."

In the preceding pages we have made use of the speeches, letters, messages, and other public documents, which furnished personal traits and anecdotes, and the book is as complete as it could be made.

THE END.

THE
UNIVERSAL MIRTH-MOVER,
AND
GREAT STOREHOUSE OF MERRIMENT
FOR THE UNITED STATES,

"YANKEE NOTIONS,"

THE FUNNIEST COMIC MONTHLY IN AMERICA,

EDITED BY THE FUNNIEST OF FUN-LOVING EDITORS,

Illustrated by a World of Comic Artists,

Is published Monthly, in advance, on the first day of each month, from the

Office of Publication of "LINCOLN'S ANECDOTES,"

105 Fulton Street, New York,

AND IS FOR SALE AT ALL BOOKSTORES AND NEWS STANDS,

And by all News-venders on Public Railways.

www.ingramcontent.com/pod-product-compliance
Lightning Source LLC
Chambersburg PA
CBHW022028080426
42733CB00007B/767